Power Through Perfected Ideas

Power Through Perfected Ideas

Notice to Readers

This book is a translation, and while the publisher has made every effort to ensure accuracy, minor grammatical or typographical errors may be present. If you identify any such issues, please feel free to notify the publisher at the email address provided below.

The publisher expressly states that there is no intent to offend any reader and assumes no legal responsibility for any errors contained within this book. This disclaimer serves to inform readers that they are engaging with a translated work, and some variations from the original text may occur. The publisher sincerely apologizes for any inaccuracies and welcomes reader feedback to enhance the quality of the translation.

Copyright Notice

First Published: **2025**

Book Name: **Power Through Perfected Ideas**

Author: **Gyanind**

Price: **250/-**

ISBN: **9789359578019**

Published: **DD Books**

Email: **ddsalesglobal@gmail.com**

Website: www.ddbookshub.com

Table of Content

Preface

"This book originates from extensive teaching experience spanning various ages, professions, and levels of education. Students' needs range from self-confidence, observation, memory, and originality to various forms of expression like conversation, speech, elocution, drama, oratory, music, and writing. It also covers aspects such as managing people, voice training, physical grace, health, and personal effectiveness in different situations. Addressing such diverse needs might seem daunting, but there's a fundamental remedy that can help in various ways.

Our aim is to make this remedy clear without delving into intricate details about its relation to human activity or different professions.I want to express gratitude to students and friends whose trust, openness, interest, and enthusiasm have greatly contributed to my happiness and any progress achieved. Each one of them should accept these words as a token of my heartfelt appreciation and fond memories."This revision maintains the essence of the original text while improving readability and clarity.

Philadelphia

February 25, 1911.

Preface to the Fifth Edition

The destiny of individuals and the progress of civilization hinge on personal education. While there's a singular theory of education, in practice, there are two approaches to teaching. The first merely imparts information, while the second nurtures all aspects of a person's being, fostering organic knowledge and developing refined ideas.The former type of teaching doesn't empower; it weakens mental and spiritual faculties, hinders personal and professional growth, and erodes civilization's foundations. Conversely, education rooted in organic knowledge achieves five essential objectives: it teaches effective utilization of existing knowledge and innate abilities, fosters a thirst for deeper understanding, enhances inherited talents, broadens the realm of the subconscious mind, and facilitates soulful expression.In simpler terms, education built on refined ideas awakens and fortifies human capabilities, orchestrating them into a powerful unified force. It instructs individuals on how to concentrate their entire being's energy on the task at hand.The cornerstone of this education, and the solution to human challenges, lies solely in organic knowledge—knowledge that thrives and evolves throughout life. "POWER THROUGH PERFECTED IDEAS" seeks to elucidate the fundamental principles guiding the acquisition of this knowledge.Note: To enhance the book's utility, the author has included one of the educational outlines applied at Neff College, Outline XV: Perfected Ideas, at the end.

The Problem

The world we inhabit presents a captivating spectacle. Each element—objects, forces, laws—holds its own fascination, and when viewed collectively, they create an overwhelming effect. Nature's intricate mechanisms, its adaptation to support life, its beauty, unveiled wonders, and hidden mysteries all stir profound reactions within us.Yet, in many ways, the Earth and its offerings serve as raw materials in human hands. Man's ability to enhance and refine upon nature adds a new layer of intrigue, opening doors to boundless possibilities. While improving plant and animal life might seem the pinnacle of human achievement, it pales in comparison to the loftier goal of self-development.Throughout history, humans have not only acknowledged the potential for self-improvement but have actively sought to surpass their ancestors and exceed their own previous accomplishments.

However, these endeavors, often lacking scientific rigor, can only take partial credit for human growth. The true drivers of personal development lie in the application of mental and physical labor, the pursuit of knowledge, the struggle for survival, and efforts toward personal, commercial, and national progress.There are assertions that individuals in certain societies are experiencing mental and moral decline. While this may not be conclusively proven, there are signs that lend credence to this notion. It's possible that the nature of work in these societies has reached its limits in fostering mental growth, or that certain segments of the population have too much leisure time, hindering their intellectual development.Conversely, the expansive scale of modern business activities has led to the cultivation of desirable mental traits, although not uniformly across all fields.

While specialization has its merits, it also tends to narrow one's focus. In contrast, the traditional worker, engaging in various tasks, or the artisan crafting goods independently, experienced broader mental growth, albeit perhaps lacking the technical expertise of modern specialists.Given the frequent discussions about the need for higher levels of mental development, it's worth briefly outlining areas where improvement is necessary. Broadly speaking, these areas encompass original intellectual capacity, a deeper and more practical understanding, and increased proficiency in various skills.In this age dominated by science, there's a growing recognition that everything follows scientific principles – there are no accidents, and everything occurs due to cause and effect. Efforts are underway everywhere to uncover and utilize the laws governing the attainment of desirable outcomes.

However, this trend has only just begun to extend into the realm of human thought and life.Human inadequacy becomes evident in our struggles with everyday problems. For instance, we've only recently begun to explore the deeper causes of happiness. We often find ourselves perplexed by our shifting moods, feeling like helpless victims of our emotions. Understanding the science of human happiness is a novel concept.Even the most socially adept individuals would struggle to articulate the principles guiding their social interactions, unaware that such laws exist.

Similarly, successful merchants, while acknowledging psychological influences on their achievements, might not be able to scientifically elucidate these factors, relying instead on practical rules they've found effective.The matters of right and wrong conduct also captivate the minds of thoughtful individuals. Various explanations, both superstitious and superficial, have been proposed to account for immorality. What are the underlying laws governing moral behavior? Why do some individuals act morally while others, under similar circumstances, act immorally? And why might the same person behave morally one day and immorally the next? These are complex questions that demand exploration.We often speak of the elusive quality of human attractiveness, of personal charm. Yet, despite its allure, individuals find it challenging to articulate the underlying principles behind this coveted trait. Some may argue that understanding the reasons behind one's charm could diminish its magic. While this may hold true if the reasons are superficial and artificial, it wouldn't apply to a deep, scientific comprehension of the laws governing attraction.Now, let's delve deeper into a more fundamental aspect of human life and assess our capacity at one of its critical junctures. Why do some individuals continue to experience mental growth for many years while others of the same age begin to decline? How do some manage to maintain a vibrant mind that evolves alongside their advancing years? And when a mind starts to weaken prematurely, why isn't its decline halted, thus postponing mental aging?Humanity finds itself adrift, pulled in various directions by countless trivial pursuits that distort and hinder character growth. There's still no widespread acknowledgment of a unifying principle or a shared ultimate objective that all can strive towards for personal fulfillment.

The world is plagued by numerous problems, many of which can only be remedied by greater mental prowess and enhanced human wisdom. It's imperative to recognize that the attainment of this higher level of development is feasible. Throughout history, there have been extraordinary minds whose brilliance stemmed from continuous growth and evolution. Inherited aptitude is a product of previous generations' development, and even mental acumen resulting from diverse genetic backgrounds relies, to some extent, on this principle of development applied differently.

Just as plant cultivation follows scientific principles, so too should the development of humanity, the pinnacle of creation. Even within conventional educational settings, there are instances of significant improvement in mental faculties, albeit often achieved inadvertently, without a deliberate focus on fostering mental growth. While all minds naturally progress to some extent through life's ordinary activities, the laws of mental development are frequently applied inadequately

.However, if the underlying causes of brain growth were comprehensively understood and systematically applied—if not only educators and parents, but all individuals became adept in this paramount science, and its principles were consistently implemented from childhood through old age—then we could expect to witness a proportionately higher level of growth and mental prowess across society.

Man's situation is indeed peculiar! Early in life, he becomes self-aware, endeavors to understand himself, and catches glimpses of the marvels within his body and mind. Yet, just as he reaches the threshold of understanding, he's met with discouragement as everything turns into a mystery. Minerals, plants, and animals live in blissful ignorance; must man remain in the dark about himself? Shouldn't he seek to know himself better? A mechanic comprehends his machine; why shouldn't man understand himself? A florist delights in the blooming of a new flower; shouldn't his knowledge of his own mind, which contributed to the flower's existence, surpass that of the flower itself? A professor masters Latin, but can he decipher the true wonder—the brain of his student? Everywhere else, everything is understood; must man alone remain an enigma?

Unbeknownst to him, man has inherited himself, giving rise to both gratitude and regret. Should he accept his current state, flaws and all, without striving for improvement? Is there no method to cleanse his imperfections or guide his evolution? Despite his lofty aspirations and inner drive, does he face perpetual dissatisfaction and inertia?

However, the path forward is as glorious as the present condition is dismal. The Creator has provided a magnificent solution for human liberation, countering the puzzling neglect of the past. For humanity's greatest need, there exists a perfect remedy. Nature's laws of human development offer the key to man's earthly destiny, providing compensation for disappointment, fulfillment of hope, and rectification of every flaw. Through their complete realization, man will embrace a noble purpose, find solace in a coherent way of life, and move towards approximate perfection—a goal for which all existence strives.

Human Efficiency

When evaluating the worth of a person's life, we can assess them from three perspectives: as an individual, in their interactions with others, and in their relation to their work. True success encompasses these three dimensions. Is the person successful in their personal growth, in their relationships with others, and in their professional endeavors? The first aspect—personal growth—serves as the foundation for the other two. If a person fulfills their potential in terms of physical health, mental acuity, and moral character, they are likely to excel both in their work and as members of society.

There's widespread consensus among thoughtful individuals regarding the physical, mental, and moral qualities necessary for a successful life. Good health, stamina, and vitality, coupled with a well-rounded intellect and a strong character, form the bedrock of success. A complete mind encompasses various faculties such as observation, imagination, emotion, memory, reasoning, and will, all functioning optimally. A fully developed mind is one where these faculties have reached a high level of proficiency.

The harmonious interaction of these mental faculties gives rise to what we term character. This includes traits like personality, authenticity, truthfulness, honesty, thirst for knowledge, originality, vision, self-confidence, moral courage, initiative, ambition, emotional intelligence, enthusiasm, appreciation, gratitude, happiness, open-mindedness, freedom from materialism, cultural refinement, balance, and inner peace. These qualities collectively contribute to a person's success and fulfillment in life.

While there's widespread agreement on the importance of having a healthy body, sharp mind, and strong character, various theories exist on how to achieve these attributes. These theories stem from differing views on the nature of the human mind and differing definitions of character, education, and knowledge. Some believe it's possible to possess an ideal mind while having an imperfect character, particularly if the mind is erroneously perceived to comprise only intellect, memory, and will, excluding imagination and emotion.

This misconception about the mind leads to other erroneous conclusions, such as the idea that personality, self-reliance, honesty, and other character traits exist separately from the mind. It's also mistakenly believed that having an ideal mind doesn't necessarily equate to knowing how to utilize it effectively or that perfect education can be misused. However, these statements are contradictory because the mind itself is the user of the mind—it's the essence of the individual. Therefore, if the mind is unable to utilize its faculties effectively, it's considered imperfect.

To assert that a person succeeds due to their personality is essentially saying they succeed because of their mind; different aspects of the mind reinforce each other. Personality, like character, is an integral part of the mind.

Similarly, suggesting that a person can be good despite having a weak mind isn't as flattering as it might seem. Their goodness is shaped by their weak mind and thus lacks the depth and richness of genuinely positive qualities. For instance, someone lacking imagination and certain emotional capacities might struggle with traits like self-confidence, tact, kindness, gratitude, and worship, as these aspects of character rely on a well-rounded mind.

There's a notion that a perfect character might sometimes exist alongside a diseased body. It's argued that even lifelong invalids can exhibit not just negative goodness but also positive virtues and a high level of spirituality. However, it can be demonstrated in such cases that as the body fails to function properly, the mind also suffers, affecting certain aspects of the individual's character. For instance, someone with poor blood quality, a weak heart, and nervous disorders would likely experience a corresponding decline in courage, initiative, and ambition.

Since all facets of character stem from a complete mind, the key question becomes how to attain such a mind. While reflecting on the importance of character traits, reading about their significance, and understanding their potential benefits are valuable endeavors, they don't fully address the fundamental challenge of achieving mental growth, developing personality, and cultivating character.

Man

Everything you do, you do with your mind. The stronger your mind, the greater you and your work will be. Enhance your mind, and you enhance yourself and your work. The most crucial type of knowledge is the one that guides you in improving your mind. Where can we find this knowledge? It lies in understanding the nature of the object you want to improve. Just as we apply the laws of plant life to grow plants and the principles of animal or human life to improve animals or educate people, we must learn what kind of being man is to discover the laws of human improvement.

Man is not like buildings, which are constructed. Instead, he's more akin to plants or animals that grow. Made things are organizations, while growing entities are organisms. Organizations and organisms share one similarity: they both require something to be added to them for improvement. However, they differ in how this addition is made.

An organization, like a wall, grows through accretion, where stones are added to the outside or top without changing the inner nature of the wall or the composition of the stones. On the other hand, an organism, such as a tree, enlarges by adding to the inside through absorption or assimilation. The sap that nourishes the tree flows up through the roots and is distributed to various parts, each portion becoming part of the tree and growing into different elements like leaves, bark, limbs, blossoms, and fruit. This process is growth by assimilation, where each part loses its identity and becomes integrated into the whole organism. Plants, animals, and humans—all organisms—grow through assimilation.

An organization, being lifeless, cannot independently grow or enhance itself. Living organisms, on the other hand, have the ability to significantly increase their growth. The higher an organism is on the scale of life, the more it can accomplish. As the highest being, man possesses the greatest potential. Among his future accomplishments in science, invention, and education, what he achieves for himself will be his most significant accomplishment.

Seed Perfection

Is man one organism or two? Does his mind grow separately from his body, or do they develop together, like a rosebush? The body and mind are inseparable, forming a single organism. Man is a unified entity. To understand his growth, he must be viewed not as two distinct parts, but as a cohesive being.

When improving an organization, such as a house, we address each part individually, addressing repairs according to each part's needs, whether it's the foundation, frame, or roof. Fixing the roof won't correct issues in the foundation. However, in organisms, there is a central life force or principle that, if properly nurtured, enhances the entire organism. In plants, this central power is the sap, while in lower animals, it's the blood. Improving the quality of the sap benefits the whole plant, and enriching the blood improves the overall health of the animal.

Since man is a single organism, encompassing both body and mind, the central force must animate and regulate both, directly or indirectly. This principle determines the growth and strength of the complete mind, the overall control of the body, the value of human labor, and the advancement of the human race.

At the core of this central power lies the mental impression or image. Understanding what a mind picture or impression is in its basic form is straightforward. When we observe an object like a clock, we form a mental picture of it. Similarly, after hearing the sound of a bell, we can still hear it in our minds even after it stops ringing. Touching a piece of ice leaves a lingering impression of its coldness in our minds long after we've removed our hand.

So, we have two fundamental elements before us: seeds and fruits. Mental impressions act as seeds, while a person's character and achievements represent the fruits. The core germ or principle leads to outcomes in human lives and endeavors. Now, let's ask ourselves: are the fruits satisfactory? Are people effective? Do they possess complete minds? Are they as morally upright as they should be? Do they attain the success they aim for in their careers? If not, could the deficiency lie in inadequate mental impressions?

Let's assume that the fruits are generally imperfect. People, on average, may not have complete minds, and they may not always achieve the success they desire personally, socially, professionally, or commercially. With this assumption, let's examine human mental impressions. If found wanting, we'll not only link human shortcomings to this source but also seek remedies.

Mental impressions resemble photographs, capturing images of objects in the world around us: buildings, flowers, mountains, and people. The crucial question is whether these mental photographs accurately reflect their subjects. If they do, then we need to explore other causes for human weaknesses and sources of greatness. To evaluate these mental photographs, we need a standard for comparison. So, we must establish what a perfect mental photograph would entail. Then, we'll assess the average mental pictures people have against this standard to gauge their correspondence.

Consider a mental picture of a bird as an example. A perfect mental photograph of a bird would encompass its correct shape, some aspects of its light and shade, and perhaps its size. Similarly, evaluating an ordinary card photograph would involve examining its shape, size, color, light, and shade. However, even with these elements, the picture wouldn't be a complete likeness because a real bird comprises numerous additional elements beyond these basic features.

Among the elements that constitute a complete representation of a bird are color, light and shade, form, size, dimension, perspective, location, direction, distance, motion, sound, odor, taste, touch, temperature, weight, hardness and softness, resistance, and more. Now, consider this: while an oil painting or a photograph captures only a fraction of the bird, the human mind, if developed and educated properly, can do much more. It can create a mental image that encompasses the entirety of the bird. Imagine a perfectly developed mind forming a mental picture of a bird. This image wouldn't be flat like a photograph or a painting. Instead, it would include the bird's movements, the texture of its feathers, the temperature of its body parts, the sounds it makes, the weight of its body, and much more. It would even extend to representing internal organs, muscles, bones, blood circulation, brain, and nervous system, with all their characteristics. In essence, this mental image would be a complete representation of the bird, both inside and out, capable of mimicking all the bird's actions and even more—a spiritual bird existing within the realm of the mind.

Now, with this perfect living mind picture of a bird as our ideal standard, we have a clear benchmark against which to assess man's mental impressions. When we say that his impressions should match the objects they represent, it becomes evident what we mean. For instance, when a person visualizes a bird in their mind, they should be able to mentally perceive all aspects of the bird as they would if they were holding the actual bird in their hands. Similarly, if they conjure an image of a horse in their mind, they should experience all the sensory details—sight, sound, etc.—as if they were observing a real horse with keen attention. Likewise, when imagining the Alps Mountains, their mental representation should encompass everything one would perceive while actually traversing the mountains—a grand, lifelike vista complete with colors, sounds, smells, and sensations of temperature. Even the internal aspects of the mountains, invisible to the eye but inferred from knowledge, should be vividly present in the mind's eye.

With this standard, we can gauge the degree of perfection of the mental impressions forming the core of the human organism's central power. As any object in the material world is composed of elements similar to those found in a bird or a mountain, we now have a universal measure to assess the quality of mental impressions.

Indeed, certain elements are more noticeable in specific objects than in others. For example, one wouldn't typically associate odor and taste with a piece of glass, whereas they would be prominent features of a flower or a peach. Even if a piece of glass were pulverized and thus emitted some odor and taste, these sensory attributes would remain less significant compared to other elements. For the purpose of mental growth, focusing on such less important aspects wouldn't be highly beneficial.

Substitutional Thinking

In evaluating the perfection of our mental impressions, we must be cautious of a subtle pitfall. Paradoxically, although a person may appear to be thinking about an object, they might not actually have a specific mental image or impression of that object. This poses a risk of assuming that one has a clear picture of the object being thought of, when in reality, there might be none at all. Consider the sentence, "Mr. Chamberlain's house in Labrador burned down last night." While you comprehend the sentence and seem to be thinking about Mr. Chamberlain's house, initially, you might not conjure up an imaginary image of this specific house. Instead, your thoughts might generalize impressions of other houses you've seen.

Although this manner of thinking conserves mental energy and serves a purpose in certain situations, it becomes problematic when dealing with important lines of thought. It's a serious error to allow this kind of thinking to replace the vivid imagination required to form a special image representing the object being considered. However, it's acceptable to temporarily employ this type of thinking until you determine whether the ideas and their purpose warrant the creation of specific mental images. This ability to temporarily use impressions and ideas as substitutes for those we lack, we call Substitutional Thinking.

To summarize the situation: When the burning of Mr. Chamberlain's house is not particularly significant to the reader, they should employ substitutional thinking. However, if it holds great importance, substitutional thinking should be avoided. Instead, the reader should construct a mental image representing this specific house in the condition and circumstances described by the sentence. Some individuals may effortlessly visualize this image, while others might initially struggle to do so. In such cases, the ability to form mental images can be developed through mental growth.

The danger lies in relying too heavily on substitutional thinking when, in fact, we should be enriching our minds and enhancing our permanent mental capabilities by creating additional images and refining new ideas. For reasons that will become evident as we progress, it's crucial not to assume, as is commonly done, that having vivid mental images of various houses or objects means we possess a vivid impression of any particular house or object mentioned in literature or elsewhere. Those who can effectively utilize both types of thinking and discern when to employ each have attained a high level of mental prowess and possess invaluable scientific knowledge.

Using a perfect impression as our benchmark, let's further examine our typical impressions to determine their alignment with what they are meant to represent. Suppose a person wishes to evaluate their mental image of the City of London. They must then pose questions about their impression of London, keeping in mind the standard impression of the bird. They shouldn't merely consider if they can think of London substitutionally, but whether they possess a distinct mental image of that specific city—one that accurately portrays London and no other city—and how closely this picture matches the standard in terms of its elements.

Assuming they have such a mental picture, they should inquire whether they can envision the entirety of London as a full-scale city. Does their mental image include many of London's likely colors? They should further question themselves: "What colors are prominent in the Parliament Buildings?" "Can I hear the sounds of London?" "What sounds do I hear in the Bank of England?" "What is the route from London Bridge to Hyde

Park?" "Can I visualize the internal workings of London?" "Do I perceive the operations of its institutions, factories, schools, shops, and law courts as vividly as if I were physically present and observing them?" If their mental image of London encompasses all these elements, then their impression is perfect to that extent. This same principle applies to all external and internal elements.

Assuming we've now completed this hypothetical test across various external and internal elements, let's pose the crucial questions: How close to perfection, on average, are our impressions? Do they include all the necessary external and internal elements according to the standard?

These are among the most significant questions we can ask ourselves. On average, our impressions of things we've observed contain only a small percentage—perhaps five or ten percent—of the elements. For things we've merely heard or read about, the percentage is even lower, and for the most subtle X-ray elements, it's barely one percent.

It's feasible to supplement these missing elements in our average impressions, thereby enhancing them significantly. We'll explore the impact this improvement can have on our mind, character, and work.

❁❁❁

Seed Growth

Impressions and the mind, in general, can be enhanced not only by adding the missing elements but also by unveiling a law through which their power can be further amplified. Let's illustrate this principle with an analogy: Picture a hundred thousand soldiers of average mental and physical caliber scattered across the country, with only one soldier in each location. Now, imagine a general aiming to transform these dispersed individuals into a formidable army. Initially, the directive is to develop each soldier physically and mentally into an ideal warrior. Upon completion, it's discovered that each individual has become significantly more adept as a soldier, equivalent to several times their previous effectiveness. Their minds are sharper, their hearts more fiercely patriotic, and their bodies possess greater skill and endurance with weapons. This enhancement of the individual soldiers mirrors the improvement of imperfect impressions in the human mind, as outlined previously.

But can we further augment the fighting prowess of these men? Despite their individual perfection, if they remain isolated and scattered, they do not constitute an effective army and would fare poorly in battle. In their dispersed state, it would take only a few properly trained enemy soldiers to defeat the entire hundred thousand.

Hence, these hundred thousand soldiers must be unified to form a cohesive army, and in this united state, they must be trained according to the principles of organized warfare. Once this consolidation and training occur, the fighting capability of the hundred thousand men will be magnified manyfold. Similarly, we may elevate each of our scattered impressions to the hundred percent standard, accomplishing wonders for ourselves. Yet, there's another significant step to take. These perfected impressions must be amalgamated through the law of association to form interconnected groups of impressions or Perfected Ideas. Subsequently, these perfected ideas must be integrated into a complete mind, a unified, organized army of perfected ideas capable of acting individually or in concert as circumstances demand.

An ideal army resembles an organism, a formidable fighting entity, steered by a central force embodied by the commanding general. Similarly, the ideal mind, composed of refined impressions seamlessly combined into perfected ideas, is a potent organism of influence governed by a dominant purpose. The degree to which impressions can be amalgamated by association hinges on their possession of elements like color, sound, etc. Since underdeveloped impressions contain only a small percentage of these elements, they can only be combined to a limited extent.

Imagine a man with a thousand average undeveloped impressions, each containing about ten percent of the elements and associated accordingly. When any one of these impressions is utilized, the man would be driven by the energy of that single impression, marginally reinforced by the energy in the few connected impressions. Now, if each of these thousand impressions were perfected, he would be propelled by a hundred degrees of energy at any given time. Moreover, if they were all closely associated such that when one impression is activated, the entire thousand reinforces it if desired, then he would be impelled not just by ten or a hundred degrees, but by thousands of degrees of energy, significantly amplifying the effectiveness of his endeavors.

True education is underpinned by a single fundamental principle, which can be likened to centralization. Firstly, it involves imbuing each mental impression with a nucleus, consolidating within it all the relevant elements like color, etc. Secondly, it entails connecting each of these impressions in a similar manner, centralizing within them all the other impressions and associated groups of impressions or ideas pertinent to that particular impression or nucleus. In essence, it entails centralizing elements in impressions and incorporating all feasible impressions and ideas into the same impression. The central impression or nucleus, along with its associated impressions and ideas, forms a perfected idea.

Beginning with the external world, various material forces such as heat, cold, and motion converge and concentrate in the human mind as impressions. These impressions then further centralize within the brain, intertwining with one another to form ideas. A complete mind is characterized by possessing an adequate number of refined ideas. The primary reason behind the shortcomings in education, and consequently in human life, is the neglect of this principle of centralization across all fields of study. Without integrating this principle into teaching, learning, thought processes, and daily life, other attempts to address issues will inevitably fall short.

God, Universe, Man

We're presented with four key points: Man, his growth through the development of his mind, the maturation of his mind via perfected ideas, and the refinement of ideas through the elements reaching the brain via the senses and the law of association.

The entire process of the universe's elements reaching the mind is known as observation or perception. Nature, from which these raw materials derive, has always puzzled humanity. The origin of existence remains a profound mystery, even if we attribute it to an Infinite Power. Nevertheless, it provides a starting point for our understanding. The universe, comprising countless worlds, is the realm upon which observation and imagination operate, supplying the building blocks for mental growth.

Living beings, including plants and animals, rely on nature for sustenance and development. The level of growth attained by each organism corresponds to what it absorbs from nature. Plants primarily absorb basic elements like temperature, moisture, and light, while animals assimilate a broader range of elements such as sound, odor, motion, and taste, making them more advanced life forms. The capacity to absorb from nature varies among animals, with some, like dogs, being more adept at it than others, like worms.

Man not only absorbs more elements than animals but also assimilates more of each element. Certain animals, due to their lifestyle needs, develop specific senses to a higher degree than humans, such as the dog's sense of smell, the eagle's sight, or the acute hearing of certain animals. Man's superiority lies not just in the quantity of elements absorbed but also in the superior associational elements, although animals possess this to some extent. Just as plants and animals vary in their levels of development based on the elements they absorb, the diverse degrees of human capabilities can be traced to the same source.

The universe is the creation of an intelligent Being, and His modus operandi seems to imbue His creations with His own nature. Offspring inherently resemble their parent; similarly, the universe, as the child of God, reflects this likeness. Plants, although seemingly separate at birth, remain connected to their parent, Nature, for sustenance. Animals, despite a perception of separation, cannot survive without remaining connected to nature. Likewise, humans, while capable of separating from their human parents, cannot disconnect from their natural parent. All living beings depend on nature for sustenance and existence. However, nature itself cannot exist apart from God; thus, we are all interconnected with the divine.

This interconnectedness implies that the more of us there is, the more of God there is. God embodies truth, and the degree to which we embody truth corresponds to our connection with Him. Plants represent truth to the extent of their existence, animals embody more truth than plants, and humans incarnate even more truth than animals. Plants and animals have evolved to their current states, capable of further growth with human assistance. Similarly, humans are capable of further evolution and growth in alignment with truth.

We nourish ourselves on God, which is truth. The elements are manifestations of God flowing through our senses, enriching our souls with divine truth. Let us rejoice in color, light, sound, odor, and all the other divine gifts. Observation is the divine influx into our lives, enriching us with more of the divine essence. It's a multifaceted process through which elements from nature and God reach our souls, transitioning from what is considered material to what is considered spiritual.

Trees draw their sustenance from their surroundings, with everything in them, except their life essence, originating from the soil, air, light, heat, and moisture. Similarly, humans inherit the life principle in embryo form. While the process of nourishing the body and converting food into muscle and bone is remarkable, feeding the soul with divine manifestations and transforming them into human thought, truth, and spirit is even more extraordinary. "The heavens declare the glory of God, and the earth shows His handiwork." Nature is sacred, and every aspect of it serves a divine purpose in human life.

A Perfected Idea of a River

A perfected mental impression is the immediate aim of the external forces acting upon us. Through observation, objects are imprinted onto the mind, and each mental image is meant to be linked with every other picture and idea in the mind. The mental realm should mirror the physical world, akin to a duplicate of earthly reality. This marks the initial phase of education.

Another vital aspect contributing to the growth of ideas is the mental environment. Just as a tree grows from a seed within its physical environment of soil, moisture, light, and air, perfected ideas sprout from a mental landscape. For instance, envisioning a rosebush serves as the core of the rosebush idea, which must be nurtured within a mental landscape mirroring the physical environment where a real rosebush thrives. The richness of the rosebush idea hinges upon the vividness and completeness of this mental landscape, extending from the immediate surroundings to the horizon, encompassing all elements, colors, and atmospheric conditions.

Similar to how a river draws water from a vast area, the development of the river idea relies on a comprehensive mental depiction of the surrounding landscape. To visualize the river's entirety, one must first envisage the entire stretch of land through which the river flows. An eighteen-element river concept can only manifest through an eighteen-element concrete foundation.

To enhance the reader's comprehension of how observation, imagination, and association contribute to perfecting any subject, let's briefly outline the river idea. We'll consider the scenario of developing the concept of a river not for oratorical or literary purposes, but rather for personal mental growth. Whether you're an author, a professional, or someone invested in personal development, possessing a thorough understanding of the river idea is crucial. However, the specific professional application or level of detail required in explaining it to others is beyond the scope of this book. When applying the suggestions regarding the river idea, each aspect should be vividly imagined both externally and internally, without resorting to substitutional thinking for any significant aspect of the subject.

Imagine a forest-covered mountain, its southern side carpeted with thick layers of dead leaves. Towering above the tree line, its summit is veiled in ice and snow, while similar peaks extend northward, forming a stark and desolate panorama of white. At the mountain's base lies an undulating plain stretching for hundreds of miles, disappearing into the hazy horizon. Beyond this lies another range of mountains, followed by a vast expanse of agricultural land stretching for two thousand miles until it meets the sea.

On a warm, nearly cloudless June morning, the mountain air is infused with the earthy scent of the forest. A gentle breeze whispers through the leaves of the trees, while in the distance, the cheerful chirping of squirrels and the melodious songs of birds fill the air. At the foot of a solitary tree stands a shallow hollow in the ground, nestled amidst fallen leaves. From the upper side of this depression, clear drops of water trickle down, gathering in a tiny basin before spilling over its edge. The resulting stream meanders downward, hesitatingly navigating around small obstacles and disappearing beneath decaying foliage, only to reappear moments later, reinforced by another similar stream. A foot below, it approaches its first precipice, cascading into a small pool with a barely audible splash. Here, a fleet of leaves drifts aimlessly, propelled by the wind. Once again, the water overflows, continuing its journey down the mountainside. A few yards downstream, the stream doubles in size, its pace quickening as it winds around tree trunks, zigzagging among scattered rocks, filling deep crevices, and overflowing its banks. Along the way, numerous smaller streams converge with it until, at last, it enters the vast plain below.

Stretching out on either side of the brook are vast expanses of green meadows, seeming to reach up almost to the horizon. Along the winding stream, groups of cattle graze peacefully, while colonies of insects make their homes in the water and along its banks. As the brook winds its way onward for a few more miles, signs of human habitation begin to appear: farm buildings dot the landscape, fields of growing grain sway gently in the breeze, and a small village comes into view. Further along, the stream enters a narrow valley, where a towering concrete wall has been erected, diverting its waters for irrigation and industrial purposes. Here, the once humble brook, now deeper and wider, nears the mountains, and is christened a river. With increasing momentum, it flows gracefully through level landscapes, gradually picking up speed as it enters the mountain passes. Rushing through deep gorges, cascading over precipices, and enduring many days of similar trials, it emerges from the mountains, ready for its final journey of two thousand miles. Along the way, it is joined by brooks, creeks, and other rivers, its path weaving through densely populated areas, sometimes narrow and deep, other times broad and shallow. Eventually, its shores disappear from view as it merges with the vast expanse of the sea.

Thousands of miles of ever-flowing water! From humble beginnings to a majestic end! Picture its ever-changing movements, coursing from mountain peak to ocean, transforming with the seasons—lush and vibrant in spring, bountiful in summer, resplendent in autumn, and serene in winter's embrace. Experience its varied moods, from the warm rush of youth to the icy grip of winter's chill. Witness its encounters with diverse weather patterns, temperatures, and climates, its voice echoing in a myriad of tones—from the gentle drip of its infancy to the mighty roar of its fullness.

The river's deafening roar echoes as thousands of tons of water plunge over the precipice.

Where did the river originate? Ask the ocean, inquire of the sun, of heat, of evaporation, of the clouds, of the wind, of gravitation, of the rain.

On its surface, at its birth on the mountain peak, float bits of bark and dead leaves; in the valley, a light canoe glides effortlessly, and beyond the mountains, on the plains, ocean liners and battleships of steel navigate its currents! By the little stream at the foot of the mountain peak, a herder's tent stands tall; by the brook, a quaint cottage; by the creek, a bustling town, and along the river's shores, vast cities stretch out into the distance. Deserts and death valleys, once barren, now flourish beyond imagination. Its generated electric energy illuminates vast swathes of country on both shores, transforming night into day; ten thousand factories hum with activity, and a million happy homes thrive; endless lines of railway transport products of factory and farm, while in Pullman palaces, untold multitudes journey, both summer and winter; a vast territory is cleansed, beautified, and transformed, doubling a nation's wealth and population.

And so, across the continent, each with its marvelous peculiarities, its ever-changing experiences of cold and heat, of sound and silence, of turmoil and peace, of destruction and blessing, rivers have flowed for unnumbered centuries and will continue to flow for ages to come, shaping the landscape and influencing every aspect of human civilization.

Rivers have not only permeated and influenced every material aspect of civilization but have also left an indelible mark on the human mind and heart. They have played a significant role in man's scientific and aesthetic development, sparking visions of wealth, igniting ambition and hope, attracting multitudes to their shores, sometimes leading to disappointment, but often inspiring and fulfilling with dazzling realization.

While these immense material waterways fulfill their purposes, their counterparts in other domains are paralleling or even surpassing the rivers in the vastness of their destinies. Among these are streams of the moving atmosphere, of the flowing clouds, of the rays of light from the sun's reservoir; there are broader streams of plant and animal life steadily advancing; streams of people from home, community, tribe, and nation, flowing, expanding, diverging, and converging; of bird, insect, and animal migration; of commerce and business, of manufacturing and transportation, all intertwining, intersecting, and intersecting again. There are the currents of progress in science, discovery, invention, education, art, and religion, with its various denominational tributaries. Human life is a stream, whether wide or narrow, long or short, shallow or deep, sometimes turbulent, sometimes tranquil. Mental development begins modestly and widens into a powerful current, flooding and enriching the landscape of the mind.

All streams and rivers everywhere, literal and figurative, material, mental, and spiritual; scientific, aesthetic, commercial, educational, moral, and religious, and the river ideas in human minds where ideas have been perfected, are all in simultaneous motion; the rivers on the mountains forever starting, the same rivers in the ocean forever ending; the unceasing life in between; birth, life, death, in rhythmic, synchronous progression; the magnificent flow of the ages; the river of the ever-moving universe; the spectacle of the laden worlds, all flowing together and forever into the ocean of the infinite.

❅❅❅

Perfected Ideas

If the river idea has now reached a stage of development where it will continue to grow spontaneously, generating new thoughts and associations as long as the brain remains healthy, then the primary objective of perfecting ideas will have been achieved.

Following the same principle, other subjects such as mother, country, peace, liberty, art, city, progress, culture, etc., can also be perfected. The individual's knowledge, facts, scattered impressions, and experiences regarding any subject can be brought to life, organized, and transformed into ideas. His understanding of a subject will then exist in his mind not as vague, disconnected information but as a living, centralized knowledge organism. Any idea that grows in this manner will connect itself with many others, thus expanding and combining indefinitely.

For instance, once the idea of progress is perfected, it can be intimately linked with the developed idea of a river to form a single compounded idea that can serve as either the idea of a river or of progress to a great extent. Under the same conditions, this compound idea can become an integral part of other ideas such as education and civilization until the entire mind becomes one great synthetic idea.

In perfecting and solidifying an abstract subject, a similar approach is taken, except that the internal qualities of the subject are typically embodied in an imaginary person or in a personified material object, and its outward manifestations are depicted through the actions of the person or personified object under the influence of the idea.

It is not implied that every idea must be as fully perfected as the idea of the river outlined here, but all impressions relevant to the success of a person's personal, professional, or business life should be perfected. Furthermore, this statement should not be narrowly interpreted, as the life of an ideal business or professional person encompasses a wide range of ideas not directly tied to their vocation. The broader a person's perfected knowledge, the closer they will be to the ideal and the greater their chances of success.

One of the significant advantages of applying this law of study is its eventual time-saving aspect. While perfecting the initial ideas may demand considerable time, subsequent ideas are refined more swiftly and with less conscious effort. Ultimately, as the mind becomes more complete, much less time and effort are required. This efficiency stems from several scientific reasons.

Firstly, the general outline for perfecting ideas applies broadly to all subjects, akin to how trees grow based on similar principles. Secondly, ideas share commonalities, often overlapping, so elaborating on one idea partially perfects many connected ideas simultaneously. Thirdly, perfected ideas tend to remain in memory, reducing the need for repetitive learning.

A perfected idea isn't merely a fleeting thought or vague notion but a substantial mental construct, an intricate organism of impressions. Mental development involves nurturing this organism by perfecting the nucleus and integrating all related impressions through association.

The nucleus of a perfected idea, like that of a river, encompasses the impression of the river from source to ocean. Surrounding it are connected impressions and ideas. While no single illustration can fully capture the experience of possessing a perfected idea, analogies like a telegraph or telephone system or a closely woven fabric are suggestive.

Imagine numerous nerves converging to form nuclei, with the entire network of brain nerves, nuclei, associated impressions, and ideas vibrating harmoniously. This vibratory momentum propels the individual towards specific objectives. All minds grow based on the nucleus and associations principle. The disparity between a substitutional mind and an ideal one lies primarily in degree rather than principle. However, this difference in degree is vast, complex, and consequential, making it practically a difference in principle as well. A substitutional mind remains incomplete.

In most lives, circumstances lead to the development of at least one, often several, highly developed ideas. With proper scientific training at the right time, these developed ideas could be duplicated and further perfected in others. However, due to the lack of necessary instruction at critical stages, many minds eventually succumb to the path of least resistance, resorting to substitutional thinking. Instead of progressing, mental activity stagnates, revolving in circles and repeating itself.

Similar to a landscape teeming with various vegetation, ideas about the same thing vary in degrees of growth across different minds. Two individuals observing the same object may not acquire equally comprehensive impressions. For instance, a child encountering a river for the first time might form a small, vague, and simple impression compared to that of an experienced traveler who has navigated numerous large rivers. The child's limited ability to form associations is due to the simplicity of its river nucleus and its scarce repertoire of other ideas for association.

A fundamental law of mind growth dictates that the degree of perfection of new ideas aligns with the existing state of growth of those already in the mind. We could refer to a person's average ideas regarding growth as their standard ideas. Individuals tend to adopt as their standard the ideas supplied by the accidental circumstances and experiences of their lives. This marks a critical period in any human life. If the standard is low and remains unaltered, all new ideas will adhere to this low standard. However, through special development, the standard can be elevated. Before embarking on any course of instruction for their life's work, individuals should apply the laws of mind development to their existing ideas, significantly expanding their average growth and raising their standard.

The value of his proposed vocational course will be immeasurably enhanced. A person with a fairly average mind, living in one place and not engaging in much reading or traveling, will have a low standard of ideas. Unless his ideas are deliberately developed through focused scientific effort, this low standard will persist. Simply reading and traveling won't significantly elevate his standard of ideas. Conversely, an individual born with a brilliant mind, who actively reads and travels, will naturally develop a higher standard of ideas without needing specialized training, although not as high as what can be achieved through scientific methods.

Perfected Ideals

There are two levels of ideas in the developed human mind: a basic level and a higher level. The first level comprises ideas of things as they exist, formed mostly through observation and partly through imagination. These are called ideas. The second level consists of ideals, which are ideas of how we wish things to be, created mostly through imagination and reflection.

At a certain point, let's imagine a person's mind has absorbed all possible knowledge from the world, and their ideas have been properly organized through the law of association. At this stage, the individual's development is shaped by the power of their ideas. But does growth stop here? Is there nothing more to be done? Fortunately, at this juncture, a higher level of ideas emerges.

While the material world usually provides the basis for the first level of ideas, the second level is primarily sourced from ideas themselves. When an ideal is successfully put into practice, it becomes known as an idea, leaving the term "ideal" for concepts not yet implemented. For instance, the kindness we exhibit today was once an ideal. As we evolve, our ideals of kindness also advance, although we may not yet fully practice them due to their imperfect state.

Perfect ideals, like perfected ideas, are practical and applicable. The effectiveness of our actions corresponds to the level of perfection of our ideas. The same principle applies to all actions, whether material, moral, or aesthetic, guided by our ideals. Some individuals merely contemplate what they should do, others discuss it, and some take action. These different expressions result from varying levels of development of the ideals prompting them to think, talk, or act. Ideals and ideas follow similar laws of growth. To be practical, we must perfect not only our ideas but also our ideals.

It's commonly assumed that people struggle to live up to their ideals because they are too lofty. However, the challenge lies not in the height of the ideals but in their imperfect development regarding their elements and associations. It's just as natural to practice a perfectly developed high ideal as it is to adhere to a perfectly developed low one. Conversely, it's difficult to apply a very imperfect low ideal. For instance, if our ideal of honesty is as fully developed in our mind as the idea of unkindness, being honest becomes as natural as being unkind. In other words, it's easy to live by a high, perfected ideal and impossible to apply a low, very imperfect one. If our ideal of kindness were more perfected, we would naturally become kinder.

Often, we lecture and advise people about what they should or should not do. However, if we only offer advice without addressing the level of development of their ideals, little progress may be made. While good advice can be beneficial, it's essential to apply the laws of perfecting ideals to strengthen weak ideals when advice alone fails.

Let's imagine that the reader holds a high but underdeveloped ideal of kindness. Although they recognize subconsciously that they should be kinder, their ideal lacks substance and is merely a collection of vague thoughts about kindness. Using their imagination, they should vividly picture a highly developed individual living and embodying a life of kindness. By associating many other ideas and ideals with this image of a kind person, especially ideas about the benefits of kindness, they can strengthen their ideal.

Let's start with a scenario: In a large city during midwinter, the streets and buildings are blanketed in snow. The reader can complete this scene by envisioning a specific setting. For instance, on one street stands a fine red brick dwelling. A tall man, dressed in a gray suit, ascends the front steps. Leaving behind the responsibilities of his significant commercial endeavors, he enters the house and warmly greets his wife and family. Quickly noticing his wife's exhaustion despite her efforts to conceal it, he insists on taking over household duties. During dinner, his warmth and kindness are evident in various gestures. Later, he receives news of his bookkeeper's sudden illness, visits him briefly, and promises to check on him the next day.

With this initial scenario in mind, the reader can continue to imagine the man's actions in various situations where kindness can be practiced. Once this imaginative exercise is complete, the reader can apply the law of association. The goal is to strengthen the nucleus of the ideal of kindness to such an extent that the reader, having perfected the ideal, feels compelled to put it into practice.

While a perfectly imagined nucleus of the ideal might lead to some positive actions, reinforcing it through association is crucial for generating a strong impulse to act kindly, even in challenging circumstances. What specific results and advantages should the reader associate with this ideal? Let's explore some of the more personal outcomes.

If the reader's mental growth were solely determined by ideas, it would have its limitations. However, where growth from ideas ends, growth from ideals begins. Since there's no limit to the growth of ideals, there's boundless potential for development. By perfecting and practicing ideals, one not only benefits oneself educationally but also serves others.

Ideals also have a significant impact on health, as will be elaborated later. Understanding the various ways in which ideas affect the body and its functions reveals that higher ideals offer greater health benefits.

Additionally, positive ideas, when perfected, contribute to the beauty of expression. Therefore, the effect of ideals in enhancing beauty is even more pronounced. For instance, a person who is mostly honest appears more beautiful than someone dishonest, but if they embody the ideal of honesty, their beauty of expression further increases. Ideals, residing in the realm of relative perfection, significantly influence personal beauty. The ideal of kindness, in particular, enhances the expression of the human face, body, and voice.

Ideals can be either repellent or attractive, with the ideal of kindness possessing strong attractive power. Embracing this ideal enhances the reader's ability to attract others, as discussed in chapters XXI and XXII.Considering the relation between perfected ideas and thinking outlined in chapter XIII, it's evident that ideals enhance intellectual power.

Moreover, since ideals are especially reinforced, they amplify emotional power, leading to a greater willpower and strength of character, as discussed in chapters XVII and XX.Culture embodies the artistic, refined, and relatively perfect human life. Therefore, a person with highly perfected ideals embodies a cultured life. Ideals refine all aspects of one's life.

Furthermore, ideals, being inherently aesthetic and forming a legitimate aristocracy in the mind, foster self-respect.

Perfected ideas manifest not only in action and life work but also in character. Similarly, ideals, being of a higher grade than ideas, result in a higher quality of work.Since ideals can influence every aspect of life, their cumulative effects signify a new and elevated existence.

Moving on to external advantages, a person's influence over others stems from their ideas and ideals. The greater the perfection of one's ideals, the greater their influence.

Ideals and ideas are instrumental in shaping success. A person's perfected ideals gradually elevate their business to a relatively perfect state.

Social relationships are influenced by a person's ideas and ideals. Notably, the ideal of kindness holds significant sway as a social factor.Similar principles apply to political outcomes, as a person's values and ideals shape their political impact.

A person's worth is determined by their character, relationships, and abilities, with ideas and ideals forming the core of character.

Many spiritual qualities stem from the cultivation of ideals. The ideal of kindness, for instance, plays a key role in nurturing profound religious sentiment.

For many, life loses its luster as familiarity breeds contempt. However, individuals with perfected ideals find inspiration in all things, perceiving the true glory in every object and condition.

The approach outlined for reinforcing the ideal of kindness can be applied broadly to perfect any ideal. For example, a person seeking to become more systematic can cultivate a perfected ideal of system and order, gradually embodying these qualities. Similarly, someone aiming to enhance honesty can develop a more robust ideal of honesty, leading to greater integrity. It's important to note that overcoming long-practiced bad habits with new perfected ideals may take time and persistence.

❁❁❁

The Perfected Mind

The ultimate goal of perfecting ideas and ideals is to cultivate a complete, vivid, and synthetic mind. A synthetic mind is one where ideas, thoughts, emotions, and ideals are closely interconnected, forming a unified whole. A vivid mind is one where impressions are as real and clear as the world outside. To understand this concept better, let's embark on an imaginary journey high above the earth.

Imagine yourself traveling miles into the sky until you reach the center of an immense empty sphere, representing your mind before it contained any ideas. Now, how do you educate this mind? Education here means filling it with something meaningful. Initially, you find nothing around you, but then you notice a bright object far below, resembling the earth you left behind. You attempt to bring the earth into your mind sphere but realize it's impossible.

Returning to your empty mind, you suddenly notice a beautiful lawn beneath your feet, surrounded by trees, horses, and people. At first, you think you're dreaming and haven't left the earth. However, upon closer examination, you realize this landscape is similar to earth but different in many aspects. This unexpected scene in your mind sphere suggests that your trip to earth somehow contributed to it. Before your journey, there was nothing here, and now there's a detailed landscape, indicating the impact of your experiences.

As you contemplate settling on the landscape in your mind realm, you recall the joy of your journey to earth and realize you were happier there than in your mind realm. This prompts you to embark on another journey to earth, where you stay longer before returning. Upon your return, you notice three significant facts: you enjoyed the second journey more, your mind landscape grew in your absence, and you realize your mind realm is your own miniature universe.

Comparing your mental world to earth, you observe that while the objects in your mind realm resemble those on earth, they are fundamentally different. Earthly objects are solid and heavy, whereas those in your mind realm lack tangible substance. Although they appear solid, they lack weight. You distinguish between them, labeling earthly objects as material realities and those in your mind realm as mental or psychic realities.

Realizing the importance of furnishing your mind realm, you decide to dedicate your life's energy to this endeavor. You also assess your means of receiving goods from earth, examining your senses to ensure you receive what you order in proper condition and promptly. To test this, you compare a material rosebush on earth to the mental bush you ordered, discovering that your mental bush is incomplete, indicating a need for improvement in receiving and manifesting desired aspects of reality in your mind realm.

As you conduct further tests on buildings, horses, and impressions of friends ordered from earth, you notice the same discrepancy—your mental objects lack many elements compared to their earthly counterparts. Recognizing that this deficiency dampens your satisfaction in your mind realm, you realize the need for improvement to prevent dissatisfaction. Understanding that your higher enjoyments must come from your mind realm during times at home, you prioritize repairing your transportation facilities.

After addressing your transportation deficiencies and making additional journeys to earth to bring up missing parts of your furnishings, you experience intensified pleasure in your home as you now receive complete objects. You also observe that the more complete objects you obtain from earth, the greater your enjoyment. Motivated by this, you continue shipments to enhance your pleasure. Eventually, you successfully import a large part of earth, excluding certain man-made things you deem valueless or harmful. Consequently, your home interests deepen, and you realize that the enjoyment of earth excursions contributes to the pleasure of your mind realm.

During one journey to earth, you discover various means of communication and travel, such as country highways, railroads, telegraph lines, and telephones. Intrigued by this, you examine your possessions to identify similar avenues of intercourse between them.

You discover that your mind realm lacks proper channels of communication, but you realize you can remedy this by constructing pathways that allow instant communion between different parts of your realm. These instantaneous messages become sources of immense interest, enjoyment, and benefit, enabling you to focus the combined force of your realm on any task you wish to accomplish.

Further, you find that just as the earth is charged with electricity, so is your realm, including buildings, animals, and people, imbued with a potent power that you can utilize in various ways for great profit to yourself and others.

Initially, your mind realm resembled a duplicate of the earth, but over time, you notice unique creations appearing—strange landscapes, buildings, cities, plants, art, music, literature, inventions, and even new people. These additions enhance the richness and diversity of your realm, making it not just a duplicate but also a place of originality and beauty.

One of your greatest joys is being simultaneously present on earth while living mentally in your mind kingdom. You derive pleasure from both realms, and each enhances the enjoyment of the other. Using your mind power, you seek to benefit yourself and improve conditions on earth.

On earth, there may be unpleasant conditions that trouble others, but they cannot reach you in your realm. You possess an entire universe that defies description—a realm untouched by decay, immune to harm from moth or rust, impervious to the influence of people or external conditions. This realm grows ever more potent, more exquisite, more captivating with each passing day. And perhaps most astounding of all, this universe is an integral part of who you are.

❁❁❁

Imagination

The so-called mental faculties aren't distinct powers of the mind but are simply what ideas and ideals can accomplish. The more developed the ideas, the stronger these abilities or faculties become. When ideas are weak and underdeveloped, there are certain tasks they cannot fulfill; some faculties may practically cease to exist, resulting in an incomplete mind.

Impressions formed through observation are essentially copies of things in the external world. These impressions serve to delight humans and give rise to material manifestations like buildings, machinery, etc., for practical benefit—both for themselves and others. However, humans have created many things that aren't mere replicas of natural phenomena. For instance, inventions aren't direct copies of nature. So, where do humans get the impressions to guide them in inventing? It's evident that humans possess another means of forming impressions apart from observation.

This additional means lies in the realm of imagination. Ideas don't just associate with each other, akin to buildings connected by telephone lines; they also blend together, much like how blue and yellow colors mix to create green. This process of blending ideas to form new ones is what we call imagination. Imagination serves as the trailblazer of invention and discovery. While observation is vital for personal growth and contributes significantly to human progress, imagination belongs to a higher echelon and achieves much more for civilization. Imagination picks up where observation leaves off.

Before humans can execute any new action, create a new object, or make progress in any field, their imagination must first visualize the action, construct the object, or envisage the advancement. All original work is thus done twice—once within the mind and then externally. Physical labor is essentially the offspring of its mental precursor. Mental exertion is the cause; manual labor is its effect.

The central challenge of life and civilization lies in nurturing the human mind to possess the capacity to envision and execute all that is beneficial for human existence and the world at large within its mental laboratory.

Some individuals possess a remarkable capacity for imagination to a greater degree than others due to the degree of perfection of the ideas or ideals they form through observation. Essentially, the strength of one's imaginative prowess hinges upon the strength of their observational skills. In simpler terms, the more refined and perfected the ideas obtained through observation, the greater the potential for imaginative creativity. The number of ideas generated through imagination is directly linked to the quantity and quality of ideas acquired through observation. In essence, the power of constructive and creative imagination is contingent upon a robust foundation of observation.

In relative terms, the primary function of observation or perception is to furnish the raw material for the creations of imagination. Therefore, our ability to imagine and innovate owes a great debt to the quality of ideas gleaned through observation.

❋❋❋

Thinking

The world outside the mind consists of objects ranging from vast entities like worlds to minuscule ones like atoms. However, it encompasses more than just these physical entities. When we observe a tree growing from the ground, a picture hanging on a wall, or a chair standing in a room, we notice something beyond the mere presence of these objects. What exists here alongside the tree, ground, picture, wall, chair, and room? These are what we call relations.

Relations denote the various connections between objects, and there are diverse types of relations that exist. Some of these relations have specific names. For instance, the tree touching the ground exemplifies the relation of contact, while the tree being above the ground signifies the relation of position. Conversely, the ground's relation to the tree includes being under the tree, touching the tree, and producing the tree—the latter representing the cause-and-effect relationship. Furthermore, the mutual relation between the tree and the ground involves them touching each other, indicating mutual contact, or being parts of a farm, representing the relation of part to whole.

Just as there are relations between objects in the external world, the mind, to some extent, mirrors this external reality. Hence, there are relations between ideas and between different components of the same idea within the realm of the mind. For instance, if I have a mental image of a parlor, within this image, there might be a mental picture of an oil painting. The relation between my mental image of the parlor and the painting is that the image of the parlor contains the image of the painting, signifying the relation of thing containing to thing contained. Additionally, both the image of the parlor and the painting are parts of my mental image of a house, demonstrating the relation of part to whole.

These connections between various contents of the mind are what we call thoughts. Recognizing or uncovering these relations constitutes thinking. Essentially, a thought represents a form of association, and thinking is one method of associating ideas. There exist numerous forms of thinking, each involving distinct ways of linking ideas together.

What determines great power in thinking? To illustrate, let's consider my mental image of a music room containing a mental picture of a piano. What influences the number of relations I can uncover, the quantity of thoughts I can generate regarding these mental images?

The determining factor lies in the elements present within my mental pictures. For instance, if my image of the piano is black and my image of the music room is white, there exists a relation of color between them. Consequently, I can formulate the thought, "The parlor and the piano are of different colors." This thought arises because each of my mental images possesses the element of color. Without color in these images, I wouldn't perceive the relation between one being white and the other black, and thus, I couldn't have conceived the aforementioned thought. Hence, the greater the number of elements my ideas encompass, the more thoughts I can generate. Therefore, significant thinking power hinges upon the perfection of ideas and ideals.

Thinking about ideas and their relationships is often termed reflection. In essence, thinking and reflection convey similar meanings. When we reflect upon ideas, we detach them from their emotional charge. The more flawless our ideas, the more we engage in reflection, and the more valuable our reflective process becomes.

❀❀❀

Memory, Recollection, Concentration

If ideas were fleeting and faded quickly from the mind, there would be a constant loss of knowledge and mental strength. This would make human advancement, significant achievements, and even happiness largely unattainable. Greatness relies on the accumulation of power without significant loss. To achieve this, once acquired, ideas must persist in the mind. This ability to retain ideas is memory. To effectively utilize this accumulated power, attention must swiftly shift between different parts of an idea, and between different ideas or groups of ideas. This is recollection. The principles governing a good memory and perfect recollection are identical.

Vivid ideas are more likely to endure in the mind. The more vivid the ideas, the more associations can be formed between them, enhancing the power of recollection. For example, the vivid mental images of our homes are seldom forgotten. If all ideas were equally vivid, we would rarely fail to recall any desired idea. Therefore, any method aimed at improving memory and recollection must focus on enhancing the quality of ideas.

The ability to hold an idea in the mind for as long as necessary or to follow a lengthy train of thought without straying is valuable. This is known as attention or concentration. The law of concentration and attention is that we can only think of an idea as long as it continues to resonate. Consequently, concentration relies on well-developed ideas. Similarly, a logical sequence of associated ideas, if highly developed, will maintain attention more consistently and with less wavering than if the ideas comprising the train of thought are weak.

Note: While the topic of Will logically follows, it is better comprehended after reading chapters XVII to XIX, inclusive.

❁❁❁

A Human Locomotive

Ideas and ideals, whether operating individually or in combination, shape the success and destiny of humanity on Earth. Understanding their nature can provide insight into how they function, aiding in their management and development. Consider a new locomotive in a workshop. While it's a remarkable machine, it's useless without additional components. It requires something to guide its movement and a force to propel it. A track provides guidance, while steam power propels it forward. Without one or the other, the locomotive is of no value.

Now, envision a physically perfect young man on the threshold of adulthood. If his mind were absent, he would be motionless, akin to the locomotive before it's placed on the track and before steam is generated. To become useful, he needs both something to move him and something to direct his movements—a guiding principle and a propelling power. These elements reside in his mind. Upon the return of his mind, he becomes akin to the locomotive on the track with sufficient steam. His actions are propelled by inner power, guided by his principles. Unlike the locomotive, both the guiding principle and propelling force for humans are found within the mind, specifically in ideas.

When we say human steam is feeling or emotion, we refer not to the sensation of emotions but to the energy they carry—the life force that propels us forward. In essence, feeling serves as the energy that drives human action.

❁❁❁

The Track

Indeed, man surpasses a locomotive in complexity, and the guiding and propelling principles within the mind have numerous facets and applications. Alongside wisdom, intelligence, and knowledge, aspects of the guiding principle include commonsense, thinking, reasoning, and judgment. Likewise, the propelling principle encompasses energy, enthusiasm, heart, ambition, inspiration, emotion, and will.

Both of these mental powers, which direct human actions and provide the energy for all endeavors, reside within ideas. Consequently, ideas possess two aspects: a cognitive side, characterized by intelligence and reasoning, and an emotive side, characterized by feeling, emotion, and energy. The connections between ideas or parts of ideas are thoughts.

Given that most people's ideas are only around ten percent perfected on average, it means that both aspects—the guiding intelligence and the propelling power—are similarly underdeveloped. Thus, improving ideas enhances both our cognitive abilities (our "tracks")—such as thinking and reasoning—and our propelling power (our energy, ambition, etc.). Improving one aspect of ideas consequently enhances everything, including the entire mind, the individual's life, and the progress of civilization.

To clarify the aspect of the guiding principle dependent on impressions, consider these illustrations: A skilled cabinetmaker, possessing well-developed ideas, sees a new design desk in a showroom. He mentally captures a vivid image of the desk and uses it as a pattern to construct a similar desk at home. Similarly, a man travels along a twenty-mile road with a friend who forms a complete mental image of the journey. Months later, relying on this mental image, the friend navigates the road alone without getting lost.

Indeed, the accuracy of the mental images greatly influences the outcome of our actions. If the cabinetmaker had formed an imperfect mental picture of the desk, his resulting creation would have mirrored that imperfection rather than matching the desk in the window. Similarly, if the friend had not observed the road closely on his initial journey, his mental image of that stretch of road would have been vague, leading to uncertainty during his subsequent journey.

Individuals who excel in their tasks typically possess perfect mental images of what they are doing. Conversely, those with imperfect mental images struggle to achieve perfection in their work. The key to improving one's work lies in refining their mental images or impressions. The principle governing flawless work is simple: perfect impressions lead to perfected ideas. When a person's ideas are flawless, everything they undertake guided and propelled by these ideas tends to be flawless as well!

❁❁❁

Steam

Many people, when they see an express train rushing by, mistakenly attribute the power to the locomotive itself. It can be challenging for the mind to correct this misconception and understand that it's actually the hidden steam that provides the energy for the train's movement. In reality, the locomotive does nothing in terms of exerting force. Consider all the different types of engines connected to various machinery worldwide—transportation systems, manufacturing plants, steamships, weaving looms, elevators, planning mills. Mentally visualize the swiftly rotating wheels of these machines and the powerful engines driving them. Yet, in none of these scenarios is there any inherent power. Disconnect the steam or other power source, and you'll witness a gradual loss of momentum until everything falls silent. Similarly, if the power of feeling were suddenly removed from people, they too would become motionless and silent.

Not only does the steam in an engine do the work, but the amount of work performed depends on the degree of steam power applied. Where there is greater power, more work is accomplished. Think about the immense power needed to haul a freight train compared to the minimal force required to run an electric fan. Likewise, in different people, there exist varying degrees of emotional power. Contrast the achievements of individuals like Napoleon or Leonardo da Vinci with those of ordinary men.

Unfortunately, few individuals grasp a clear understanding of cause and effect, even in the material world. Therefore, it's not surprising that even fewer perceive the law in the world of the mind. The phrase "I did it" is commonly used, but its understanding is often as flawed as saying "The elevator lifts the people." For most people, "I" refers not to the guiding and propelling principles of the mind but to their physical bodies, with little consideration for their minds. This misconception hinders a correct understanding of human nature. Recognizing that it's the mind, not the body, that drives our actions represents a significant step towards scientific self-knowledge and self-development.

Human life provides daily examples demonstrating that the mind, particularly the aspect known as feeling, plays a significant role in all types of successful work, often more than is commonly recognized. Great work, defined as work performed correctly from a psychological standpoint, relies as much on the worker's feeling as on their intelligence. One individual infuses their work with heart and feeling, achieving not only superior results but also carrying out their tasks spontaneously and without a sense of drudgery. In contrast, another person approaches their work without heart, viewing it as dull, burdensome labor, resulting in products that fall below their potential standard. The type of feeling known as inspiration has the power to alter the course of human history, influencing victories and defeats in battles. In education, it is equally crucial to nurture and strengthen students' feelings as it is to impart knowledge. Teaching and learning methods that neglect the development of ideas, focusing solely on accumulating facts regardless of the quality or perfection of the underlying ideas, fail to promote the holistic cultivation of students' emotional lives. Moreover, they weaken the innate sense of feeling inherited by students.

❁❁❁

Replenishment

Ideas perform their work for man through a process akin to the operation of an engine, although this analogy is not meant to be scientifically precise but rather illustrative.

Similar to how the fireman shovels coal into the locomotive's fire and replenishes the water tank when necessary to maintain steam production, two essential elements for generating human steam are food and blood. Ideas, constantly engaged in tasks on our behalf, expend their energy, akin to the consumption of coal and water in the locomotive. To replenish this energy and ensure the continuous functioning of ideas, blood pumped by the heart carries refined nutrients to the brain cells, where ideas reside. Here, the elements of ideas and the blood converge, forming impressions in a mysterious manner.

Just as coal holds latent heat when inactive but releases active heat when burned, ideas possess dormant feeling when not in use, which becomes active when they are engaged in tasks. During our waking hours, some ideas are active while others remain inactive. In this state of dormancy, both the propelling and guiding aspects of ideas are latent until they are called upon to perform tasks.

When an idea becomes active, akin to a lump of coal combusting, its dormant feeling is discharged, allowing it to perform work for us. However, unlike coal, which is entirely consumed except for ashes, only the substance supplied by the blood is consumed when an idea becomes active. The mental form of the idea remains intact even after its discharge, akin to how a grain of powder explodes but leaves remnants behind. The consumed substance is then replenished by the blood, primarily during sleep.

This process mirrors the universal law of waste and repair, supply and discharge, observed in the natural world. Just as engines, trees, and animals require a constant supply of external materials to sustain their functioning and growth, the mind also relies on an influx of outside materials to support its working capacity and development.

❁❁❁

Steam Pressure

Steam exhibits power only when it is under pressure. Observing a kettle boiling, one can witness the steam escaping through the spout. However, once the steam disperses into the air, it loses its power and becomes harmless. Yet, envision a kettle without a spout, featuring only a small hole for pouring water. If this hole were tightly closed, and the kettle filled with water, heating it would cause the water to boil and transform into steam. As more steam is generated, it fills the space within the kettle, exerting increasing pressure against its walls. Eventually, if the pressure becomes too great, the kettle may burst.

The critical insight is that steam possesses power only when it is under pressure. In the absence of pressure, it remains harmless. In the case of an engine, the boiler is designed to withstand high pressure without bursting. Once sufficient pressure is achieved, the steam is directed into the cylinder where it pushes the piston, propelling the wheels of the engine. Instead of escaping, the steam, under pressure, is now performing useful work.

Similarly, the vibratory energy of feeling, present in the brain cells, operates under pressure. It is this pressure, not just the sensation of feeling, that constitutes human power. Analogous to steam under pressure driving the engine, feeling under pressure transmits its energy along nerves to muscles, employing them as tools to perform work. Feeling without pressure lacks power, but when pressure is applied, the greater the pressure, the greater the propelling force.

When feeling under pressure is not properly relieved, the consequences can be more severe than the bursting of a kettle. Many crimes and wrongdoings in human life might have been prevented if the pressure of feeling had been given a different outlet before becoming irresistible. Understanding this law of pressure and its proper use could have directed feeling towards good rather than evil. Feeling under pressure seeks various ways to express itself or find relief. Thinking about an idea, discussing it with others, reading related materials, engaging in activities guided by our ideas, or encountering the objects that initially sparked the ideas are some ways in which feeling in ideas is alleviated.

To illustrate how feeling under pressure operates in daily life, consider a typical human experience. A young man grows up on a farm, surrounded by familiar objects, people, and activities. His mind accumulates impressions of his surroundings, and he experiences the cycle of mental waste and repair daily. Engaged in farm work, he interacts with his environment, which helps discharge the feeling in his ideas accumulated during sleep. His life proceeds contentedly without much desire for change. The same ideas and desires guide him, leading him to familiar places and activities each day. However, one day, a stranger visits the farm and captivates the young man with vivid descriptions of distant places, especially a large city. After the stranger's departure, the young man continually discusses the stories he heard, particularly about the city, signaling a shift in his desires and aspirations.

Why did the young man leave home? The pressure in his imagination of the city, fueled by the stranger's descriptions, became so intense that it compelled him to satisfy his strong desire to visit the city and relieve the pressure. The allure of the imagined city surpassed the pressure exerted by his familiar home environment gained through observation. If the pressure from his imagination had not outweighed that of his home ideas, he would have remained at home.

Why did he experience homesickness upon reaching the city? Upon arrival, part of his blood, previously replenishing his home ideas, was redirected to nourish his imagined ideas of the city, partly relieving the pressure. Another part was utilized to form new impressions of the city. However, the remaining blood continued to flow into his home ideas, which were left unused, leading to an accumulation of pressure and resulting in homesickness. His desire to return home, driven by the stronger pressure of missing his familiar environment, eventually led him back.

Under what circumstances might he have avoided homesickness? Engaging his mind in activities that required more brain blood, leaving less to replenish his home ideas, could have delayed or mitigated homesickness. Continuous enjoyable entertainments or deep involvement in meaningful work could have distracted him from longing for home.

There are two additional reasons why some individuals may not experience homesickness. Firstly, those with weak ideas are not prone to homesickness. Such individuals are content in any environment and may move about due to external influences rather than internal desires. If they return home while away, it's not necessarily driven by a strong longing. Secondly, individuals with highly developed ideas, leading to rapid mental growth, are less likely to experience homesickness because their blood is occupied forming numerous new impressions.

Homesickness essentially stems from intense desire, which is a form of pressure guiding one towards a desired object or place. If homesickness is labeled as a "sickness," why not consider any strong desire for something as a mild "sickness" for that particular thing? While not all desires reach the level of sickness, the underlying principle remains the same. Various terms like ambition are used in psychology to describe essentially the same phenomenon. For instance, an intense desire to become President of the United States could be likened to "president sickness," illustrating the scientific reality behind ambition.

An incomplete mind primarily composed of superficial knowledge, facts, and thoughts typically lacks intense pressure of feeling. Significant pressure of feeling is usually present only in well-developed ideas.

❁❁❁

Will

Will power, in this context, refers to the ability to compel oneself to complete a task or undertake an action even when there may be a lack of initial desire or interest. It is the capacity to override immediate impulses or preferences in favor of achieving a specific goal or fulfilling a necessary obligation.

In the example provided, the woman exerted her willpower to prioritize her housekeeping duties over her interest in writing a magazine article about her benevolent society. Despite her strong inclination towards the latter, she recognized the essential need to attend to her household responsibilities, particularly in preparing meals for herself and her children. Therefore, she consciously made the decision to exert her willpower and focus on the tasks related to maintaining her home and ensuring the well-being of her family.

Willpower originates from a combination of factors, including rational deliberation, moral considerations, and the recognition of the importance or necessity of a particular action. In this case, the woman's understanding of the vital role of meals in health and life served as her primary motivation for exerting her willpower to prioritize her housekeeping duties over her personal interests.

No, willpower is not a separate energy or power distinct from what has been discussed regarding ideas. Instead, it is a manifestation of the propelling energy derived from specific groups of ideas associated with a particular line of action. When individuals exert their willpower, they are essentially tapping into the emotional or motivational force contained within certain ideas or sets of ideas that are favorable to the desired course of action.

In the example provided, the woman's decision to prioritize her housekeeping duties over her interest in writing a magazine article stemmed from her recognition of the importance of meals for health and life. This understanding was accompanied by a strong emotional component, particularly as it pertained to her role as a mother. By associating the necessity of meals with her housekeeping responsibilities, she effectively borrowed the emotional energy from the former to reinforce her commitment to the latter.

Therefore, willpower is essentially the result of leveraging the emotional or motivational content of certain ideas to bolster weaker ideas associated with the required action. It is not a separate power but rather a function of the interconnectedness and influence of ideas within the mind.

Without this ability to harness the emotional or motivational force of specific ideas, individuals would be subject to the whims of whichever ideas happen to possess the greatest pressure at any given time, regardless of whether they lead to the most advantageous course of action. However, by cultivating numerous, highly perfected, and interconnected ideas, individuals can achieve a balanced and wise alignment of interests within their minds, promoting mental equilibrium and facilitating actions that serve the highest good of both the individual and society.

Two Kinds of Feelings

Indeed, just as steam in an engine serves the singular purpose of propulsion, human feelings serve multiple functions beyond mere propulsion. Human feelings can be broadly categorized into two types: pleasant and unpleasant, which can further be subdivided into various kinds. These feelings not only drive individuals forward but also serve as mechanisms for experiencing happiness and unhappiness.

Positive feelings emanate from positive ideas and result in pleasure or happiness when discharged, while negative feelings arise from negative ideas and lead to unhappiness. Understanding the roles of happiness and unhappiness in human life can be likened to comprehending bodily comfort and pain. Physical comfort and pain can be considered the happiness and unhappiness of the body, respectively, while joy and sorrow represent the comfort and pain of the mind.

The design of pain in response to disease or injury in the body serves as a protective mechanism. Pain acts as a warning signal, notifying individuals of underlying issues or harm, prompting them to take action to address the cause of discomfort. Similarly, mental unhappiness serves as a warning and a punishment, signaling dissatisfaction or imbalance in the mind.

Just as physical pain alerts individuals to potential harm to the body, mental discomfort indicates underlying issues in the mind that require attention and resolution. It serves as a deterrent, motivating individuals to address the root causes of their unhappiness. Conversely, mental happiness and bodily comfort affirm adherence to mental and physical well-being practices.

In essence, both mental and physical discomfort act as signals of potential harm, prompting individuals to take corrective action. Conversely, mental happiness and bodily comfort signify alignment with mental and physical well-being, reinforcing positive behaviors and experiences.

Our level of happiness is directly tied to the quality of our positive ideas. Similarly, the intensity of our unhappiness corresponds to the strength of our negative ideas. The more negative ideas we harbor, the more frequent our unhappy experiences, whereas an abundance of positive ideas leads to more frequent moments of joy. If we were solely influenced by negative ideas, perpetual unhappiness would ensue. Conversely, an existence filled only with positive ideas would result in continuous happiness, barring external factors causing distress. The impact of pleasant and unpleasant feelings extends to our physical well-being, affecting crucial bodily functions. Negative thoughts disrupt digestion, while positive thoughts aid it. Considering this, let's explore why negative mental states may harm health and positive ones may benefit it. Good health hinges on factors like oxygen-rich blood, which relies on proper breathing. Positive mental states and happiness encourage deep, regular breathing, maximizing oxygen intake. Conversely, negative mental states lead to irregular, shallow breathing, reducing oxygen intake. No specific breathing exercises are needed for individuals with positive and well-developed ideas. Therefore, good health is closely linked to refined ideas and ideals. Positive ideas foster harmony within the mind and body, facilitating the smooth operation of bodily functions. The heart's regular action and proper blood circulation are contingent upon positive mental states, while negative ones lead to irregularities.

These two opposing states significantly impact the appearance of the human face. A face frequently contorted by emotions like envy, hate, anger, or worry gradually becomes chronically ugly.

Transient negative states further exacerbate this condition, making the face doubly unattractive. Conversely, positive conditions give rise to a beautiful countenance. Over time, a face expressing only positive feelings assumes a permanently beautiful expression.

Negative states also manifest in awkward body movements and ungainly positions, while positive conditions foster grace in posture and movement. Discordant mental states not only affect facial expressions and body language but also the tone of one's voice. Like facial expressions, there are permanent and transient discordant tones in the voice. Positive states of mind, on the other hand, express themselves in beautiful tones.

The influence of others on our mental growth is substantial. Their respect, appreciation, and approval, whether expressed or silent, are crucial for our development. Positive conditions not only bring pleasure but also tend to inspire similar feelings in others. Our own positive demeanor attracts others to us, leading to mutually beneficial interactions that stimulate our mental growth. Conversely, negative feelings tend to inflict pain on others, leading to social ostracism. As a result, we become more negative and further isolated. Naturally, we seek out individuals or experiences that can discharge our positive ideas.

Various outcomes such as good health, beauty, attractiveness, grace, and social power all stem from positive ideas. Health attained through positivity is vibrant, robust, and enduring. Beauty originating from a beautiful spirit represents the highest form of beauty, while attractiveness rooted in soul qualities is always beneficial. These qualities are inherent in nature, making nature the true healer. Mental harmony forms the basis of outward grace and purity of tone, while positive ideas and feelings serve as the only legitimate source of magnetism. A vigorous physical and growing mental life stand as the ultimate cosmetics.

Negative Feelings

Negative ideas and the discordant feelings they generate pose significant obstacles to mental growth, while positive feelings are crucial not only for mental development but also for overall health, beauty, happiness, and influence. Therefore, it's essential to explore whether it's possible to avoid negative influences and cultivate positive ones, and if so, how to achieve this.

Negative mental conditions typically stem from two causes: underdevelopment and ignorance. Individuals with vague minds tend to allow their negative impressions to be discharged carelessly, leading to discordant feelings. They often experience anxiety, worry, and despondency, absorb negative gossip, and dwell on grim news stories.

In contrast, those with a cultivated mind of perfected ideas actively avoid negative thoughts and feelings. They consciously strive to construct and discharge only positive impressions. By consistently engaging with positive ideas, their negative impressions gradually weaken, while their positive ones strengthen. They do so because the intensity of their positive ideas and feelings makes enduring discordant emotions unbearable. They eagerly seize every opportunity to discharge positive impressions, anticipating the great pleasure that awaits them.

Undeveloped individuals may lack the strong aversion to negative experiences and the attraction to positive ones that drive more developed individuals. Their emancipation from negative influences often depends on the guidance and support of their more educated counterparts. These enlightened individuals, having experienced their own share of miseries and joys, are emotionally driven and intellectually equipped to assist their less fortunate peers, acting as their mentors and guides.

Man remains in a state of relative underdevelopment and ignorance, and civilization mirrors this imperfection. Despite gradual progress, each new generation inherits the flaws of its predecessors and absorbs some of the weaknesses of the civilization into which they are born. Despite his mental limitations and lack of scientific understanding, man endeavors to tackle the myriad challenges posed by the material world. Even from early childhood, he grapples with questions about the origins of humanity and the universe, seeking to interpret nature and its laws more comprehensively as he matures. These interpretations, often unscientific and tinged with negativity, are transmitted through literature, art, music, history, and tradition from one generation to the next. The present generation finds itself burdened with this mass of negative ideas. Should we allow these ideas to continue wreaking their destructive effects on us, as they did on our ancestors, and pass them on to future generations? Or should we strive to find a remedy for them and their harmful influences?

Many forces of nature, such as earthquakes, lightning, and storms, have been superficially and even superstitiously interpreted, leaving negative impressions on the human mind. It's often assumed that these forces are inherently negative because they sometimes result in the loss of human life. However, an alternative perspective may lead to a different conclusion. We might consider that human development is the underlying purpose of the part of the universe with which we interact—that Earth serves as a school for humanity's growth and evolution.

One of the key ways in which man develops his mind is through the exercise of attempting to understand, utilize, and control the forces of nature. This exercise contributes significantly to his intellectual growth, even if it leads to negative conclusions initially. For example, before the nature of steam was understood, it was often seen as a dangerous nuisance. However, through man's ingenuity and understanding, steam has been transformed from a destructive force into a constructive tool, representing a shift towards positive ideas. Similarly, wind, once considered largely negative, now powers ships and performs other important functions. As technology advances, even elements like air and oceans, formerly seen as negative, are becoming avenues of commerce and travel.

Despite the fear thunder and lightning once inspired, electricity, harnessed from these phenomena, now drives modern civilization. While earthquakes remain mysterious and are largely viewed negatively, there is hope that advancements in science and technology may one day enable us to predict and mitigate their destructive impact.

Disease has long been a source of negative thinking, but it is not an inevitable consequence of existence. Rather, it arises from the violation of natural laws. By working to prevent and cure diseases, humanity advances and develops. Sickness, pain, and sorrow serve as nature's penalties for these violations, prompting individuals to think critically and utilize their mental faculties. Through this process, these afflictions take on a positive character, driving human growth and development.

In conclusion, there is no negative aspect of nature that cannot be overcome through the advancement of ideas and human progress.

Words

The advancement of civilization has greatly benefited from the transmission and preservation of knowledge through printed language. However, the personal benefits to individuals have been indirect. Surprisingly, when comparing the overall mental prowess of today's most accomplished scholars with those of the pre-printing era, the former may not exhibit the expected superiority despite the advantage of access to books. Many scholars, while possessing extensive knowledge, do not necessarily possess strong mental faculties or complete minds.

Books and the invention of printing have introduced a new challenge to education: the development of the mind through language. While much of our knowledge comes from books, the value of this knowledge in fostering mental growth depends on the quality and perfection of the ideas contained within them. This, in turn, is influenced by the reader's previous development and their approach to studying books. Therefore, it is crucial to understand the laws and conditions of effective book study.

How does language in books influence association and imagination in the formation of ideals and ideas? While we can gain ideas from directly observing objects like flowers or landscapes, the process is different when we read about them in books. Books consist of words and sentences, so let's focus on words first. For example, when I look at a rose, I perceive it as an object. However, when I close my eyes, I can visualize a mental image of the rose. Similarly, when I see the word "rose" written or printed, or hear it spoken, different mental representations are triggered. Thus, we have three types of mental words: the mental image of the object, the visual representation of the written or printed word, and the auditory perception of the spoken word.

With the rose before me on the bush, the idea of the rose in my mind, and both mental and material words at hand, let's explore their relationships, utility, and interactions. The physical rose exists on the bush, while the mental image of the rose resides in my mind. The spoken word "rose" is conveyed through vibrations in the air and is processed in the brain.

When I see or hear the word "rose," it triggers my mental image of the rose, and the act of thinking about this idea partly relieves the associated feeling or pressure. During speaking, writing, or listening, words operate unconsciously, with our conscious focus typically directed towards the more engaging idea rather than the words themselves. However, if the idea is vague, attention may shift from the idea to the word.

Consider a box with a card labeled "flowers." In this case, the word serves as a label for what is contained within the box. Words like "tree," "rose," "fire," and "hope" are names or labels for specific things. These external labels, signs, or symbols facilitate communication among people but are merely mediums of exchange. For effective communication, each individual must possess the corresponding idea, mental spoken word, and the appropriate wave motion of the air to evoke the mental image associated with the word.

Sentences

Single words trigger the discharge of ideas already present in the mind. However, groups of words, such as phrases, clauses, sentences, and paragraphs, serve additional functions beyond mere discharge. While words and sentences cannot introduce external elements like color or sound into the mind, they operate with what is already present.

There are three primary effects that can be achieved with the contents of the mind: discharge of ideas, association of ideas through ordinary connections, and composition of ideas through imagination. Single words discharge ideas, while sentences establish associations and compound them. Sentences also reveal new relations between ideas and stimulate new thoughts through association, as well as form new compounds through imagination.

To illustrate, consider a prescription obtained from a doctor and taken to a drug store. The prescription serves as guidance for the druggist to assemble medicines already in the store. Similarly, sentences act as prescriptions for the mind, directing it to combine certain ideas already present. Just as medicine is obtained through a prescription, thought is obtained through a sentence. However, there are no drugs or medicine in a prescription, just as there are no ideas, thoughts, or feelings in a sentence. A sentence functions as a directive for thought, truth, ideas, associations, images, and feelings. Truth, knowledge, and facts reside in the mind, not in sentences. For a prescription or sentence to be useful, the required elements must already exist within the respective stores.

Before a sentence can have any significance, the ideas it intends to connect must exist within the mind. Similarly, if a druggist lacks a specific drug indicated by a prescription, he has two options: acquire it from a wholesale supplier or create the needed drug by combining available ones. Likewise, when a reader's mind lacks a particular idea mentioned in a word or sentence, two courses of action are possible. The reader can seek the required idea from the broader universe through observation, akin to visiting a wholesale house. Alternatively, the reader can blend or combine existing ideas in the mind to generate the needed one. For less critical matters, substitutional thinking may suffice.

Books

The role of sentences described applies equally to books. While observation forms the basis of mental photography and some association of ideas, literature primarily relies on association and imagination. Books rely on observation to provide a foundation of perfected ideas. Without the contribution of observation to the mind, books would lack efficacy. They offer two significant advantages: preserving and disseminating language, the symbols of knowledge. Through the distribution of knowledge prescriptions, books, magazines, and newspapers foster breadth in mental growth. However, if books are used unscientifically, they may hinder mental development. When sentences convey truth and moral correctness, and facilitate vital connections between ideas, books are invaluable. Nevertheless, the improper use of books can have detrimental effects on the mind's growth. Ideas develop through use and require discharge for growth. To ensure adequate exercise and growth, attention must focus on ideas. Unfortunately, improper use of books shifts attention from ideas to words, leading to a mental disorder known as the disease of symbolism, which impedes mental growth.

Another consequence of improper book usage is the expression of relations between relations, leading to weakened relational vibrations in the mind. While the ideas themselves may be adequate, they may not supply sufficient vibration for such remote relations. This results in abstract, substitutional conceptions incapable of guiding action. This has contributed to a flawed concept of education, where quantity of knowledge, regardless of idea perfection, is prioritized over quality. The traditional notion, "Knowledge is power," must evolve to emphasize the quality or perfection of ideas. The remedy lies in perfected ideas. Students must discern when their ideas are ready to engage with book language effectively. Laws guide us in proper book usage; ideas to be associated by book knowledge must be perfected and possess a high degree of feeling under pressure. This leads to a desire for their discharge and, consequently, a specific book. Reading such a book brings intense pleasure to the reader.

One may not initially feel drawn to a specific line of thought, but a well-written book can spark interest in later chapters through its early pages. If accomplished, such a book proves valuable to read. Sometimes, the desire to read a book arises from others' recommendations, yet upon reading, one may find no pleasure due to lacking necessary ideas or poor alignment with the book's content. In such cases, it's best to avoid reading the book.

Self-expression

Physical muscles, mental faculties, and ideas all strengthen and improve through proper use. In natural, varied self-expression, human abilities are optimally utilized and consequently become highly developed. Someone following the principles of the New Education will eventually find a vocation that allows for their fullest self-expression. However, no single line of work encompasses the entirety of one's potential. Alongside their main occupation, a person should engage in various other activities to express themselves fully. Those who can express themselves in numerous pursuits will excel most in their primary vocation.

From a self-growth perspective, the question arises: is it wiser to pursue a livelihood in a profession that aligns with one's deepest passions and have additional avocations for recreation and personal growth, or to pursue a financially rewarding occupation that does not fulfill one's soul? The former risks narrow-mindedness, while the latter may lead to mediocre success and unhappiness. Assuming a person's central goal is their own growth, and they have sufficient freedom in their work to exercise their creativity fully, the former path is preferable.

There are many avenues through which a person can express themselves. Being a sympathetic listener allows for the exploration of ideas that may otherwise remain dormant. There are situations where verbal expression, whether through public speaking, art, writing, or music, is essential for personal growth. Avoiding such forms of expression deprives individuals of opportunities for development.

One common reason for failing to express oneself is a lack of understanding of its impact on personal growth. This is primarily due to having weak ideas, which undermine the sense of self-assuredness needed for expression. Since the motivation to express oneself cannot arise from weak ideas, it's crucial to strengthen them in every possible way. One effective method is to associate all the benefits of self-expression with these ideas, thereby refining our ideal of self-expression. Nothing can replace the opportunities lost by not expressing oneself. Even if we fail externally, there is always internal growth because effort always leads to mental development. Moreover, increased mental strength gained from such efforts will eventually bring about some level of external success.

❋❋❋

A Perfected Idea Man

A man with a complete synthetic mind, characterized by highly developed and perfected ideas, will inevitably become a growing individual, enriched with the numerous advantages that growth brings. Growth, the most significant quality of perfected ideas and a complete mind, leads to rapid and continuous development. Such a person finds great pleasure in the discharge of perfected positive ideas, recognizing that happiness and other benefits stem from ongoing growth. Consequently, he naturally becomes deeply interested in his own growth, making it the central purpose of his life.

The growing mind also yields the fruit of original ideas, a crucial outcome of continuous growth. Just as every apple is original to the tree that produces it, a person with a growing mind generates numerous ideas that are original in nature. Additionally, through constant mental stimulation and replenishment of ideas, he maintains a position at the forefront of his time. His mind fosters courageous initiative, enabling him to confidently advocate for and apply new ideas.

Moreover, the continuous exercise of his mind in his work provides him with intellectual, moral, spiritual, and physical nourishment, thereby increasing his desire for further mental and physical growth. This growth in one direction fuels his appetite for nourishment in the same direction, creating a virtuous cycle of development and fulfillment.

Growth fosters open-mindedness, allowing one to embrace truth from any source. This openness leads to broad-mindedness, as the complexity of perfected ideas enables one to consider various perspectives on a subject. In contrast, narrow-minded individuals experience emotional discomfort when confronted with new ideas that challenge their limited knowledge, causing them to avoid new information.

Ambition naturally arises from the growing mind, as it forms images of new accomplishments and desires their realization. Positive ideas and harmonious feelings characterize such individuals, leading to beauty of expression in body, voice, and language, as well as grace of manner and action. Their entire being, including body, voice, and actions, is harmoniously guided by their mind, resulting in a psychalized, spiritualized presence.

These individuals possess wide adaptability, with the ability to synthesize and analyze, lead or follow as needed. Their highly complex ideas give rise to distinctive individuality, enabling them to offer unique contributions to the world. Importantly, their focus on ideas rather than mere facts allows them to grasp truth within their sphere of knowledge, granting them a sense of freedom within their chosen domain. Their self-confidence and self-reliance stem from the realization that they possess the power to manifest their desires through their ideas and actions, leading them to prioritize truth and ideas above all else.

The ability to envision the Earth or any part of it with clarity and to immerse oneself in positive ideas or ideals reflects a poetic mind. In this state, everything becomes idealized, and even the ordinary transforms into something captivating and sublime.

Personality encompasses all mental faculties and their activities, knowledge in its entirety, and character with all its aspects. True education, proper study, and scientific engagement enhance personality and character. A well-educated individual will have no dormant areas in their mind, with every aspect of their being contributing to their life's goals. Such a person will possess a distinctive personality and, knowing that true value lies within themselves and that happiness is within their control, will find contentment.

With a well-rounded mind and character, they achieve balance, maintaining equilibrium whether in action or in stillness, during routine tasks or significant life events. They exude a sense of calm and repose. As their mind evolves, they come to realize its superiority over the physical world, finding greater satisfaction in their mental landscapes than in material possessions. They stand as the culmination of natural evolution, the embodiment of creative power, and the steward of a remarkable estate.

The New Work

The new individual will produce work that is original, detailed, and artistic, infused with a spirit that eliminates all sense of drudgery. Just as play was a source of joy and growth in childhood, productive work now serves as a form of play. His work arises from his own nature, fitting him perfectly and contributing to his mental, moral, and physical development. As he grows, his work evolves into a fine art, improving alongside his own personal growth.

Any form of work, even the simplest manual labor, can be performed mechanically or spontaneously. The properly educated individual engages in daily labor, but they are not mere day laborers. It is not the nature of the work itself that determines its worth, but rather the mindset in which it is approached. The ideal individual does not lower themselves to their work; instead, they elevate it to their mental plane. For instance, an undeveloped person may find preaching to be a burden, while a new individual may turn quarrying into a fulfilling calling. By idealizing manual labor and recognizing it as an educational necessity and a profound blessing, humanity achieves an important outcome.

Currently, many of the world's greatest minds are drawn to commercial life due to its financial rewards. However, business transcends the individuals who enter it. Unfortunately, the average businessperson often finds themselves overwhelmed by forces that were meant to elevate them personally. This outcome is not inherent to business itself but rather reflects the mental state of the individual involved.

For a manufacturer to succeed fully, they must possess a vivid, comprehensive vision of their factory, business operations, and the market in which their goods will be used. This vision allows them to make sound judgments, seize opportunities, and even forecast future business trends. In today's complex world, where business encompasses social, moral, scientific, psychological, and philosophical dimensions, when led by individuals with properly prepared minds and diversified interests, it becomes a powerful catalyst for human growth.

The emergence of new teaching methods is both a cause and a result of the new approach to education. A fully developed human being serves as the foundation for this new teaching paradigm. In the classroom, it is essential to have teachers with complete minds who embody humanity. Unfortunately, many educators who lack such development resort to conventional practices, rigid discipline, and superficial standards of instruction when faced with challenges.

A true teacher embodies and promotes the principles of the New Knowledge. Rather than assigning tasks for rote memorization, they impart facts that have transformative power and bring messages of joy and empowerment.

Similarly, the work of a novelist is inherently creative. To craft a compelling story, a writer cannot rely solely on superficial knowledge of plot, settings, characters, and actions. Merely substituting ideas will not suffice; instead, the writer must delve deeper. While initial ideas may stem from substitutional thinking, they must be fleshed out, imagined, and depicted in vivid detail. The story should be so intricately imagined that if it were to materialize in the real world exactly as envisioned by the author, it would be complete and compelling.

Effective and artistic writing is achieved through perfected ideas and a comprehensive understanding of the subject matter. While some writers may possess innate talent, others can attain excellence through development. The essence of great writing lies beyond superficial instruction; it resides in the richness of ideas. True literature flourishes when natural-born writers are equipped with the principles of the New Education through comprehensive college training.

Many musicians envision a New Music, understanding that the essence of music lies in the harmonious vibration of feeling generated by the discharge of musical ideas. True musical expression occurs when this discharge, fueled by perfected ideas, manifests in harmonious sounds, whether vocal or instrumental. Musicians recognize that it's possible to produce pleasant sounds devoid of this soul element of music. The challenge lies in cultivating mental vibration of adequate strength and quality.

A great musician transcends mere technical proficiency; they possess a vivid, concrete conception akin to that of a great author. This level of artistic insight is only achieved in the idea mind.Similarly, individuals who pursue acting as a profession must go beyond mechanical imitation. The ideal actor doesn't superficially imitate; they fully inhabit their character, living on the stage. To accomplish this, actors must deeply understand the characters, settings, and evolving mental states throughout the performance. When this depth of engagement becomes common among actors, theater will emerge as a powerful educational force.

A natural-born orator possesses an extraordinary inheritance of the elements necessary for the growth of perfected ideas. While some may possess this talent innately, many can develop it through scientific methods. Regardless of natural talent, anyone can significantly enhance their abilities through targeted development. Perfected ideas and a fully developed mind are the keys to mastering oratory, both in its practice, study, and teaching.

The principles discussed regarding perfected ideas, concrete understanding of knowledge, and the synthetic idea mind are equally applicable to various fields beyond manual labor, business, teaching, drama, authorship, music, and oratory. They extend to art, architecture, and all trades and professions.

In art, for instance, artists must possess a deep comprehension of their subjects, envisioning and expressing their ideas with clarity and precision. Similarly, architects require a profound understanding of design principles, materials, and spatial relationships to create functional and aesthetically pleasing structures.

In every trade and profession, individuals benefit from cultivating perfected ideas and a comprehensive understanding of their field. Whether it's engineering, medicine, law, or any other discipline, success hinges on the ability to synthesize knowledge, conceive innovative solutions, and express ideas effectively.

Ultimately, the application of these principles across diverse domains underscores their universal significance in fostering growth, creativity, and excellence in all endeavors.

Some Educational Inferences

The realization of the results of perfected ideas within a single lifetime depends on various factors, including the individual's receptiveness to new concepts, their willingness to undergo rigorous training, and their capacity for growth. While it may take several generations to fully implement scientific education and witness its highest benefits, individuals of different ages can still experience significant improvements through focused study.

Children who receive education based on the idea principle from an early age are likely to reap marked benefits throughout their lives. However, even individuals who have been taught substitutionally for most of their education can still reform their minds and achieve substantial advantages through specialized instruction later in life.

For someone in their twenties who has undergone substitutional education but seeks to pursue a course of instruction based on mind growth principles, the effort can indeed lead to significant benefits. Similarly, individuals in middle life, despite their age, can be repaid for their efforts through scientific development. Age itself is not the sole determinant of the extent to which one can benefit from such education. What matters more is the individual's mindset, openness to new ideas, and dedication to thorough training.

Even individuals past the age of fifty can experience substantial rewards from adopting scientific development practices. The key lies in the individual's willingness to embrace new learning methods and commit to the necessary training, regardless of their age.

Yes, this education based on the idea principle is indeed necessary for everyone, and it is adaptable to all individuals. It is not a manufactured process but rather a natural form of education that aligns with the principles of nature. This educational approach is suitable for all branches of study, including subjects like higher mathematics, despite initial assumptions that such abstract disciplines may require a different approach.

The adaptability of idea education is further underscored by its universality, catering to individuals of all ages, from childhood onwards, and accommodating various mental conditions and vocations. Even those already established in business or professional life can benefit from specialized development without needing to delve into entirely new lines of thought. Instead, the principles can be applied to familiar impressions and practical daily use.

In the classroom setting, the success of applying the idea principle depends significantly on the motivations of both teachers and students. These motivations should be guided by the direct objectives, spirit, and nature of the work being undertaken, rather than solely by theoretical considerations. It's important to recognize that a developed mind transcends mere knowledge; it encompasses aspects that extend beyond existing or future knowledge, allowing for unrestrained growth and expansion.

The difference between school work based on the idea principle and substitutional education is significant but complex. Presently, most students approach their studies in a substitutional manner, especially in subjects like history. The question arises: how would a student prepare for history in a more concrete way?After going through the motions of studying, reciting, passing exams, and graduating, what remains of the historical facts in the student's mind? Are these facts as vivid and tangible as real-life experiences? If they are, then the student's interest and engagement would be intense. These historical facts would become as familiar and significant as memories of home, shaping the student's thoughts and actions.

However, it's widely recognized that this depth of engagement isn't typical in historical study. The problem lies in substitutional education, which focuses more on rote memorization than true understanding and application of ideas.

To address this, teachers shouldn't just assign lessons; they should guide students in preparing them concretely. This means helping students develop the ability to engage with and understand the core ideas of the lesson, rather than just memorizing facts. This type of preparation involves using imagination, making concrete connections between ideas, engaging in original thinking, and considering the emotional aspects of learning.

By studying in this manner, lessons become memorable because memory is embedded in a deeper understanding of ideas. Teachers preparing students for this approach must themselves understand and apply these principles. They should be like skilled gardeners, nurturing the growth of ideas in themselves and their students, understanding the intricacies of idea cultivation.

We've explored how different aspects of an idea enter the mind, understanding that sounds and colors originate primarily from the external world rather than from within consciousness or printed words. For instance, a young child needs to hear a sound or smell an odor to form impressions of them, and repeated exposure deepens these impressions.

Similarly, experiencing heat by merely placing a hand near a hot object gives a partial impression, but full immersion intensifies and broadens this perception. This principle extends to other senses, such as motion. A child's understanding of motion evolves from observing a speeding machine to experiencing various forms of motion firsthand, eventually comprehending the complexities of different movements.

The involvement of the entire body in forming impressions is crucial for developing certain aspects of ideas and corresponding parts of the brain and mind. A fully developed mind, enriched through comprehensive sensory experiences, possesses the ability to engage with subjects like history through the idea-based approach, even when using books and teachers in a traditional educational setting.

In essence, education conducted effectively, incorporating both sensory experiences and traditional methods, plays a vital role in nurturing and expanding the capabilities of the mind.

Studying scientific books doesn't isolate the growing mind from its primary nourishment and exercise—the universe. Instead, it complements mental development by assisting in associative, imaginative, and logical tasks while encouraging closer and more intelligent interaction with the physical world. Both in and out of school, children should engage in activities that foster mental growth and physical development across all dimensions each day.

Substitutional education falls short in this regard, as it only engages a small fraction of the mind and body during crucial stages of growth, resulting in incomplete minds, underdeveloped bodies, and a constrained civilization. In such schools, both teachers and students lead limited, mentally stifled lives that deviate from natural human experience.

True education, however, should reflect the breadth of life as it ought to be, not just as it is. Ideal life encompasses more than mere substitutional thinking, offering a broader scope for mental and physical development. Unfortunately, outdated notions of education, centered on rote learning and diplomas, often hinder efforts to cultivate intelligent freedom and positive action.

To counter this, educators strive to break the "don't habit" mentality ingrained in some homes and challenge the misconception that education is solely about book knowledge and credentials. Instead, they aim to foster a holistic understanding of life and education, promoting mental liberation, expansion, and comprehensive development.

Due to constraints like limited time and resources, schools and colleges cannot be expected to provide a student's entire education, even during their attendance. For optimal results, teachers should guide students' daily lives both within and outside of school. Educators who effectively communicate to parents the value of incorporating home life and surroundings into education, emphasizing the importance of practical skills and work ethic, serve not only families but also society and the state.

Various educational institutions, such as kindergartens, manual training schools, vocational institutions, and agricultural colleges, align with the idea principle by engaging the body in learning experiences. Classical education also holds its place, albeit to a limited extent. However, where these methods fall short of fostering holistic mind development, it's often due to reliance on substitutional instruction and preparation.

When classical and manual training approaches fully embrace the idea principle, they will maintain their essence while integrating new principles. Classical education, aiming for cultural enrichment, tends to prioritize knowledge acquisition, while manual training focuses on practical skills but may neglect character development. By reevaluating motives and methodologies and applying new principles, both approaches can facilitate greater mind growth.

☸☸☸

A Prophecy

Scientific education promises not only a transformed humanity and a new way of working but also a fundamentally different human existence. At its core is the prioritization of human growth, which will shape thought and action. As a result, many material pursuits currently deemed crucial will diminish in significance, leading to a more refined and enduring material progress. Mental, aesthetic, and spiritual aspects, currently relegated to the background, will rightfully take their place.

In this new paradigm, individuals will be valued not solely for their possessions, knowledge, or accomplishments, but for their ongoing growth. Knowledge and achievements will no longer be external attachments but integral parts of one's personality and character. Success in financial matters, scholarship, or deeds will be measured by the extent of mental growth accompanying them. Individuals will transcend their accomplishments, with their true essence reflected in the richness of their minds.

Artistic and cultural appreciation will be judged not by material possessions but by the inner treasures of the mind—soulful symphonies and mental galleries adorned with artistic creations. This shift will herald a new age founded on scientific principles, where all phenomena are viewed through the lens of the mind. The world will become a vast university, with various vocations and professions serving as departments of human development.

Schools and colleges will seamlessly integrate with daily life, ensuring a smooth transition to the larger "University of Life."

Civilization will be unified, centralized, and harmonized, with each aspect reinforcing the development of power through perfected ideas. In this envisioned future, humanity will achieve a profound synthesis, with all elements contributing to the collective advancement of society.

The End